DEDICATION

To My Precious Grandparents: Walter and Vera

I can hear you in the back of my mind, cheering me on to keep running my race, and I am sure you are doing just that with the rest of the Saints.

Thank you for the love you poured out on me throughout my life, and for the wisdom you imparted to me. I am looking forward to the day I get to hug your necks again and tell you all about the fruit in my life because of your influence. I love you Pops and Grandma.

To My Children: Matthew, Brandon and Amanda

You inspire me to be a better mom and strive for excellence. I am amazed at your tenacity in life to go after God's plan and the fruit displayed in your lives from the seed of His Word.

May you fulfill and receive all that God has for you and endeavor to leave a legacy for Christ. Know that you are most precious to me, and I love you dearly

GOD
can
TURN IT
AROUND

HOW TO PARTNER WITH GOD FOR YOUR VICTORY

PAMELA PHILLIPS

LIFEWISE BOOKS

ACKNOWLEDGMENTS

When I began writing this book, I desired to bring the message of hope, seeded deep in my heart, to a people who were standing in front of a mountain—a people striving to overcome. I had an overwhelming urgency to reach out to those who had walked through many disappointments and are stretching to grasp a thread of their hope—or for those had reached a glass ceiling and are believing for a breakthrough.

It was in this season of my new beginnings I joined a community who share similar visions of business and ministry. I reached out to a dynamic woman of God who directed me to this organization who assists people embarking in their new beginnings, and her name is Melody Barker. I am most grateful for her wisdom and creative expression, and her passionate example has changed my life.

I also want to thank David Baker for his persistence with helping me birth the dreams in my heart. The pieces to the puzzle came together and helped me simplify what was in my heart to do.

I want to immensely thank Charity Bradshaw and her team, and many others who have surrounded me with encouragement, prayer, financial support, and blessings; my gratitude is more than words can speak. All of you have made this book possible, and I am sure it will count toward your rewards in eternity as it bears much fruit.

INTRODUCTION

I believe God has given me the book you are about to read to share as a tool of encouragement to those who are embarking on a journey they haven't traveled before. This could be the season of a new marriage, the birthing of a child, the transition of the empty nester, or a promotion to a new position in a career. It could also be the pursuit of a healthier lifestyle after a bad doctor's report, a new beginning after a divorce, a new chapter after losing a job, or finding peace after a loved one passed away.

Many once served in ministry or owned a business, only to find themselves left standing at a distance when the storms of life ravished the dream once held so dear, making it appear the dream is gone. As you sojourn, let the words of this book be a seasoning of salt for your life. Your best days are ahead of you, and you will gain hope if you choose not to give up. Allow God to build upon your life with wisdom and understanding and use you to the fullest capacity for His glory. Whatever season you find yourself in, it is my prayer that you receive a gift of faith and gain new strength to put your crown on and fulfill all God has for you to accomplish.

The story of this book begins one evening as I was listening to the radio. It was a tough season for me, and I was seeking God on direction for my life. I had big questions about myself, my future, and my relationships. I was going about my routine as usual, when I heard the lyrics to a song, which inspired the birthing of this book.

The song was about how some giant taunts a person saying they will never make it. The giant laughs at the person, but instead of listening to the giant, the person listens to the voice of truth. Tough times require strong faith. Just know the storm you are weathering will pass and the best is yet to come. The season you are experiencing is an opportunity to move into something bigger God has planned for you, to make His name great, and to demonstrate to all the world you serve a mighty God. As a farmer plants his seeds and prepares for the harvest, so you must also prepare yourself for the rain and the harvest, for the good things of God, and for His favor.

As you read the pages of this book, be inspired and encouraged. Be still and know that He is God as you journey in your Promised Land and be in wonder as He unlocks the doors to your victory.

CHAPTER 1

Is There Anything Too Hard for God?

Every Problem is an Opportunity to Trust God

I have an interesting story to tell you. It was several years ago, during the time my children were young, when my husband and I decided to go all the way with Jesus—to trust Him at His Word. I was so hungry for Him and wanted to see and experience the miracles I was reading about in the Bible. The year I made that decision, I was tested, and it was one of the most challenging years I can remember. However, it was also a supernatural growth that accelerated the whole family, and I will always be grateful for God drawing me and my family to Him, and for moving us forward into His plans.

During that time, a mentor of mine invited me to a Bible meeting. My husband agreed that I should go, so I went. Right after the worship finished, a very polished and well-dressed woman who was ministering came walking across the stage and said that God wanted to do the miraculous, and we needed to step out in faith and trust Him. She looked right at me and asked if she could pray for me. I told her "Yes," and walked to the front. As she began praying for me, she asked for a young woman on her prayer team to come and lay hands on me, and as she did, she uttered a prophetic word from God to me. I began to feel a coating of warmth flow over me and the anointing of God filled me in a way I never had experienced before.

What was amazing to me is that this woman preacher of God knew this young lady had a word from God to give to me. The word of the Lord was, "God is doing a miraculous thing in your life in this season and wants to show you His power. Feel the anointing He is pouring into you. You will begin to step out in this next season to be used of God, and this anointing will flow through you like living water. God is with you and your family. God says, I am with you. Do not be afraid. Be still and know that I am God."

I went home and meditated on that word for several days. You see, that word meant a lot to me as my husband was out of work, the bills were starting to come due, and it would be Christmas in a few weeks. Even though God had done a great work in all of us and we were no longer materialistic, we still wanted to celebrate Christmas, and I wanted to give gifts to my children, friends, and family. I believed with all my heart the word I was given that day was really from God because only God knew my circumstances and I trusted Him.

Soon after that day, I was impressed from the Lord to go to a local store and I happily went with the children as I did every year. I told the kids to pick out a couple of things they would like to get and give me some ideas of what to buy. They were very modest in their selections because they knew we were on a very tight budget, and they were content to open whatever I bought. They were bringing items to me and picking items up they really liked. I was so very thankful for what God had done in our hearts, and that our focus was on Jesus. I knew God was rewarding us for putting Him first. I was so excited about how real God was making himself to our family.

I continued to pray and believe every day as I reminded myself of the divine word from God. I knew God was going to show up with a miraculous thing in my life and was expecting it every day. Three weeks had gone by, and it rolled around to just a few days before Christmas. The electricity was about to be terminated, and food was starting to run low. My close friend told me a church nearby was handing out toys and food, and that they may be able to help with the lights. I was very reluctant to go ask for help and quite frankly didn't like asking for help, but with persistence from my precious friend, I went over there to the church the last Saturday they held the give-away program.

I got there a little earlier than when I was told it began in case there was a line. A lot of people were out of work at that time, so I expected there to be a long line. However, I was surprised because there weren't any people waiting and no lines. In fact, the doors were locked to the church, and the parking lot was empty. Thoughts ran rapidly through my mind. Maybe I wasn't supposed to get help from them after all? I began to wonder if I'd missed God. I felt as though the Lord was saying, "Go around to the other side of the building." I went around to the other side, and there were three vehicles parked there, near a glass door. I went up to the door, but it was locked.

About that time, a person walked down the hall from inside the building, so I knocked on the door. A kind and gentle lady opened the door and informed me that all the toys and food had been given away because there was such a great need, and there wasn't anything left to give out, so the church had closed for the day.

I thanked the soft-spoken lady for telling me they were closed and turned around to leave, disappointed. Suddenly, that still small voice inside said, "Don't be afraid. Don't be discouraged." I had a thought to put my name and number on the small truck windshield parked by the door. I began analyzing what putting a number on the truck could possibly do and for a moment, I thought my efforts were futile.

As I stood there and thought about it, I reasoned the worst thing that could happen would be for them to say they couldn't help me. I put my name and number on a small piece of paper and left it on the windshield of the small truck as I believed God was instructing me—then went home.

I told my friend about what had happened after I got back home that Saturday afternoon and she insisted God told her I was supposed to go there. She said I should call that church back on Monday. I had agreed to go ahead and call the church on the following Monday with my friend's persistence. On Sunday however, the kind lady who answered the door at the church called me and told me she found a note on her son's truck with my name on it. I chuckled and described the events of the day before.

I told her my story about the reason I was coming to the church, as she listened patiently. She told me it was no accident we were talking or that the exact vehicle I put the paper on was her son's truck. She shared that she usually doesn't go down to the church on Saturday, but she was there because her son was doing a special project. She told me she would call me back the next day.

I still called the church Monday morning to find out if they had any programs to help with my electric bill as I was desperate. My lights were about to be shut off the next day. I wasn't even concerned about anything else at this point because the temperature outside was at the freezing point and there was ice on everything. I left my name and number with the department handling calls for assistance and was told someone would get back with me.

Much to my amazement, the same soft-spoken lady called me back and said my Christmas Angel had shown up. She was very eager to help and comforted me with encouragement and prayed for me. She explained that she was in charge of that program to assist families in need. After discussing our family situation in detail, she told me she would call me back to give me instructions and that they would also take care of the lights!

She asked me my children's ages, genders and we discussed where I wanted to meet her so she could give me some gifts for the children. I was so relieved that my electric bill was going to be paid that I completely forgot about the Christmas gifts or even about needing the food.

It was just a couple of days before Christmas when I met this sweet lady at a restaurant parking lot in the area I was living at that time. She got out and opened the back of her SUV and told me to go ahead and start taking out the packages. I saw several packages that filled the back of her SUV. I asked her to tell me which package to take and she said, "All of them. These are all yours". I couldn't get over it! I was in awe that I was unloading all these packages for my children. We loaded all the packages up in my car and then she opened the back door and told me the groceries were mine and to grab them as well.

There were two medium-sized boxes full of groceries and the amazing thing I was surprised about is they were all the exact brands we used. There was also had a huge turkey with the groceries, which was what I loved to cook at Christmas. I didn't tell her all of these details. I didn't give her the items my children wanted for Christmas or tell her what toys they like. This was a very personalized miracle from God. She then handed me a card and my eyes filled with tears as I began to read the poetic words written in the card.

This kind and mild-mannered lady became very serious as her eyes met mine and then she began to minister to me. She knew God's hand was on our lives, and she had been praying about who she was supposed to be giving these things to. For three weeks before the day I met her, people had been bringing all these things to her and telling her that it was for a family who was crying out to God, and it was for a specific person God wanted to reveal Himself to in a mighty way.

Person after person would bring her these items in the packages and the food in the boxes and tell her that God specifically had them pick that item out and it was to go to a specific family. Each toy in those packages was exactly what the children had picked out at the toy store, even down to the purple doll stroller my daughter gazed at but never asked for. When I opened the card, there was enough money to pay all the rest of my bills, gift cards to eat at a local restaurant for our entire family, and a beautiful poetic writing, "Hear the wind blow through the trees. Listen to the whisper of His voice–Be still and know that I am God."

REHEARSE PAST VICTORIES

You may be at a point in your life where it just feels hopeless. You have prayed, fasted, and stood on God's Word, but you may be wondering when it's ever going to turn around. The two words that come to my mind for this situation are, "Press in."

The Bible tells the story of a shepherd boy who suddenly finds himself facing a giant. This giant is threatening David's family, friends, and the town where he lives. As David stands before Goliath the giant, he isn't afraid to fight him. David knows this giant represents more than just the opinion of a loud-mouthed large man making threats. He is facing a threat to the community, to the peace and well-being of his family, and an attack against the kingdom of God. He has a cause to engage this heathen who is defying the people of God and God's name. At this time, David is a teenager and doesn't have the experience of fighting in the army. His brothers tell him he can't fight the giant because he is inexperienced, young, and not trained. He is made to stay in the pastures and watch over the sheep.

God trains him out in the field, preparing him for His future as king. While out in the field managing the sheep, David fights and kills a lion and bear to defend the sheep. He is skilled with the weapons God gave him as a shepherd—skills paid for through training and sacrifice.

He is able to fearlessly face those animals because he knows that not only the sheep depend on it, but his life does, too. His ability to overcome in those dangerous times gives him trust in the Lord's ability to bring him the victory, and this gives him the confidence to go stand before Goliath and fight him. He overcomes those challenges and fearlessly faces the greatest threat. Just like the sheep depend on David to defend them against wild animals, the people in his town and family need defense.

It doesn't make sense to let a shepherd boy go and fight the giant. This giant has skill, is much bigger and stronger than the men in the army, and shouts out threats every day from the mountain to intimidate the army. Day after day, the giant tells the army how he is going to kill them, how he is god, and how he hates them. He exalts himself to the point he is insisting the people worship him.

The giant's constant barrage of intimidation wears down the army of Israel, causing them to fear and become discouraged. They begin to doubt their ability to stand up to the giant and are focused only on how big and strong he is as they meditate on his cursing words. They have completely lost their focus on how big their God is. All they can think about is what this giant is telling them and how hopeless it looks.

Isn't that just how the enemy tries to deceive us? He taunts us with insults, tells us we are weak, and reminds us of a prayer that might not have been answered the way we wanted, points out how big the problem is, or says, "No one recovers from this sickness."

All creation is waiting on you to put your crown on and do what you were put on this earth to do. Is this problem you are facing too hard for God? Is His arm too short? "My righteousness draws near speedily, my salvation is on the way, and my arm will bring justice to the nations. The islands will look to me and wait in hope for my arm."[1]

THE BATTLE IS THE LORD'S

The battle is the Lord's, so praise Him. When you enter into praise, it sends a message to the enemy and causes him to have confusion. Your victory is imminent if you don't give up.

God's purposes will be carried out if we will hold fast and press in and seek His plans. We must keep our focus on moving in the path He has already carved out for us. We absolutely cannot be moved from our peace. If we hold the peace in our heart and stay focused, we will be able to tap into the plans of God and will know the instructions. You will overcome. God will be exalted. Don't listen to who people say you are, but who GOD says you are. You are not defined by the opinions of people around you.

Who does God say you are? You are not defined by your circumstances. Listen to the voice of truth that says, "You are victorious in Christ." You are a child of the Most-High God. Greater is He who is in you than he who is in the world. The voice of deception will come to you and try to tell you are not worthy, you are not able, or you are limited by what you see.

He has already given you the victory and prepared the way for you. God will strengthen you and cause you to soar like the eagle if you don't give up and don't quit. Your victory is at the door and God is ready to change the season in your life if you are willing and obedient to His voice. Tell me, what is impossible for God? Is there anything too hard for God?

PRAYER

Father,

I thank You that You are always with me. Thank You for all the purposes You have for my life and for trusting me to carry them out. Father, I ask that You give me strength to stand strong in the face of the enemy, fine tune my ears to hear Your voice, and sharpen my eyes to see the path You have already prepared for me to walk in, with all the provision necessary to accomplish the task.

Help me to encourage myself when I hear the enemy taunting me with words of defeat, and to remind myself of all the victories You have given me in the past. I know that if You have brought me victory before You will do it again. Let my light so shine before men that they will see Your good works and praise You. Let my faith draw men to You for salvation. Amen.

CHAPTER 2

Fly Like an Eagle

Desire for Success Must Be Greater than Fear of Failure

Have you considered the difference between chickens and eagles? In general, chickens are followers of other chickens. They follow along in their curious and nosy investigation of what other chickens are doing. They are quite interested in their neighbors' food and quickly become jealous and fight over bugs and feed in the chicken yard.

If one chicken finds a bug to eat, all of them want it. As they wander around the yard aimlessly scouting for what the other chickens might have, they can become very fearful, too. If a storm suddenly comes with loud thunder and heavy rain, the chickens will immediately become frantic, running in circles and flapping their wings.

In contrast, let's take a look at what eagles are like. They are purposeful in their method to obtain food. They rise far above the ground to gain a higher perspective to catch their prey. The eagle does not travel with other eagles and they are deliberate with every move. The eagle is committed to what it is destined to do, without concern for what the other eagles are doing.

They are not fearful of a storm but wait for the right moment to soar when a strong wind comes allowing them to catch the updrafts. The eagle uses the adversity of the storm to create an opportunity for itself. The main difference I want you to see between eagles and chickens is that while they are both birds, the chicken is fearful and concerned with what the other chickens are doing and the eagle is not.

While this simple illustration is about birds, I want to parallel some similar habits and mentalities that we as humans maintain. As Christians and children of the Most-High God, we were made to fly above the storm like eagles. One very important lesson I learned from my mentor years ago is that the 'anointing is in the instructions.' We attract what we focus on.

The Word says, "Beloved, I pray that all may go well with you and that you may be in good health, as it goes well with your soul."[1] Your soul (mind, will, and emotions) must prosper.

The enemy will try to act clever to divert our attention towards what's wrong but remember that he doesn't come up with anything new. If we are constantly focused on the problem, then we might miss the answer because we aren't looking for it. I'm not saying we shouldn't acknowledge our problems, but rather exalt God and His Word above any problem we could be facing. Whatever we put our mind's attention and heart's affection on is where our focus will be.

One Sunday morning, my pastor was giving an illustrated message and he brought up a time when he and his wife went snow skiing. The funny thing is, his wife was gliding around on the snow and taking the hills like a pro.

My pastor, however, was not acclimated to the snow at all. In fact, he didn't know how to ski and was taking adult ski lessons. He said he felt a little awkward on the bunny slopes along with his kids learning how to ski. The one thing his instructor would tell him every time before he took off down the slope was, "Whatever direction you look, your skis will follow." If he looked to the left, his skis would turn left. He looked to the right, his skis would turn right. If he wanted to go straight, he must stay focused ahead, and his skis would go in that direction. [2]

That same principle is true in our walk with God. Have you ever gone through a season when it seems like everything is going wrong? The car needs repairs and you have more bills than money at the end of the month. Or, it may seem like it is taking way too long for your prayers to be answered while you watch everyone around you get theirs answered.

Maybe you've been praying for breakthrough for a long time, and yet, it doesn't seem to happen? In fact, distractions may have crept in and now you are so busy dealing with "other things" that it seems you will never see your dreams birthed? It may feel like the harder you press forward to obey God's plan for your life, the greater the hindrances mount up against your efforts and begin wearing you down.

YOU WERE CREATED TO FLY

Remember, if you are born again into the Kingdom of God, you are the child of Almighty God. The Word of God says,

> "When I look at Your heavens, the work of Your fingers, the moon and the stars, which You have set in place, what is man that You are mindful of him, and the son of man that You care for him? Yet You have made him a little lower than the heavenly beings and crowned him with glory and honor. You have given him dominion over the works of Your hands; You have put all things under his feet, all sheep and oxen, and also the beasts of the field, the birds of the heavens, and the fish of the sea, whatever passes along the paths of the seas."[3]

God has created you for a specific purpose. Everything you were sent to this earth to accomplish is already on God's mind before you begin to walk it out. The assignment you are on in this season has already been provided for, you just need to step into it. To keep things in perspective, the main focus here is to advance the Kingdom of God, and as a child of God, He wants you to succeed even more than you do.

When you are moving forward and obstacles begin to push you back, it can be frustrating. It's easy to get into comparison with others who appear to have it easier. The interesting thing is they may be experiencing setbacks as well even though it may not be obvious. Realizing that your Father has prepared the way for you, given you the authority to accomplish His will, and knowing you can receive His instructions will usher in the confidence you need to rise above the situation.

This confidence is grounded in who God is for us:

> "Have you not known? Have you not heard? The Lord is the everlasting God, the Creator of the ends of the earth. He never grows weak or weary. No one can measure the depths of His understanding. He gives power to the weak and strength to the powerless. Even youths will become weak and tired, and young men will fall in exhaustion. But those who trust in the Lord will find new strength. They will soar high on wings like eagles. They will run and not grow weary. They will walk and not faint."[4]

He hasn't abandoned you; He cares about you and what concerns you. He knows the very number of hairs on your head. Everything planned for you on this earth is written about you in Heaven. He has an assignment that only you can fulfill. God takes every tear you shed and puts it in a bottle. He is paying attention and cares deeply about what concerns you.

He has given you power to tread on serpents and scorpions, and over all the power of the enemy, and nothing will by any means hurt you.[5] Jesus is the Alpha and Omega, Beginning and the

End, First and the Last. He is for you and wants the best for you. All heaven is cheering you on. There is nothing impossible with God. He is with you.

SEEK GOD'S PLAN FOR YOUR LIFE

"I knew you before I formed you in your mother's womb. Before you were born I set you apart and appointed you as my prophet to the nations."[6] Now you may not be called to the office of a prophet, but God has appointed you for a specific purpose on this Earth and that is why you are here. It is no accident you are here and you are appointed to do a specific job.

Yes, there are giants in the land, and they want you to believe they are bigger and stronger than your God. Know that the lie of the enemy is only a shadow and it will fade away when the light of truth shines on it.

PRAYER

Father,

Thank You for Your promises in the Word. Thank You for always loving me unconditionally, and for never giving up on me. Please help me to keep my eyes on You and not be moved by my circumstances. It seems like it is hopeless and my faith is being tested and shaken right now. You are greater than any of these problems I am having, and I know I can trust You. You said in Your Word You would never leave me or forsake me, so I know You are with me.

Please show me what to do and how to walk in Your will in this situation to obtain the victory. Shine a light on my path and order my steps. Open the doors that You would have me walk in and close all other doors. Give me the strength to keep my focus on You, so I can soar above this storm victoriously. Amen.

CHAPTER 3
Walk with Me

Never, Never, Never Give Up

What breakthrough are you standing for? What is God calling you to do specifically for His Kingdom? God has sent you to Earth for a specific assignment. Remember that God has your back and your best interest in mind, and you will receive whatever you need from Him to accomplish the assignment. Let your trust arise in the Almighty God.

When Elisha is at the end of his life, King Jehoash of Israel comes to visit him because the King of Aram is oppressing Israel. He has been oppressing Israel for much of the entire reign of King Jehoash. Elisha tells him to get a bow and some arrows, to put his hand on the bow, open the eastern window, and shoot. Elisha tells him that this is the Lord's arrow, an arrow of victory over Aram, and he will completely conquer the Arameans.

Then Elisha tells him to pick up the other arrows and strike them against the ground. So, King Jehoash picks them up and strikes the ground only three times. Elisha is angry with him. He tells him he should have struck the ground five or six times; then he would have beaten Aram until it was entirely destroyed, but now, he will only be victorious three times. Elisha is upset because the King got weary and didn't persist for his victory. Don't get weary and stop—you could be right around the corner from your greatest breakthrough.

Persist with the "arrows," the Word of God, in prayer, and victory will be at the door. We need to keep our face like flint toward God and be determined to overcome. We will then gain strength and begin to rise above the strife and oppression that tries to hold us down.

One trick of the enemy is to subtly persuade us to stop trying. The voice of defeat will barrage our thoughts, tempting us to invite in the fear of failure. The giants of failure want to cause fear to rise inside of us, taunting us until we quit. Defeat may even appear around every corner and can seem overwhelming. I want you to know it is in those instances that God wants to use you to show just how mighty He is. He wants the world to know that He is God and will reward those who diligently seek Him. I know that God is merciful, and even though the circumstances may have been brought on by a mistake, God is faithful and just to forgive us and turn around the circumstance to bring Him glory.

STAND FIRM

When Moses brought the children of Israel out of Egypt, he heard whining and complaining. They were constantly telling Moses they were hungry and unhappy and wanted to go back to Egypt where all was familiar. Even though they wanted to go into the Promised Land, they still had the mentality of Egypt and being a slave.

They really didn't want to pay the price for freedom and didn't want to go to the next level with God and believe for His miracles. They were content with the routine and really wanted to keep doing what they had always done. God became very angry with the children of Israel and wanted to destroy them, but Moses interceded for them and God had mercy. He not only provided for their food needs, but their shoes and clothes didn't wear out!

We have a much better covenant with God because of what Jesus did at the cross. Don't you know that because you are a child of God, His eyes are on you? He loves you so much He gave His only son to die for you. I tell you my friend, He loved you so much and had mercy on you even before you thought of Him. Your coming to Him, whether it occurred at a church altar or somewhere else, happened because He drew you to Himself, and it was because He thought of you first.

WHAT IS YOUR ASSIGNMENT?

So, tell me—what is your area of influence? Are you called to stay at home and train your children to serve God? Is the marketplace your zone? Some are called to intercede for others or to preach the

Gospel. Everyone has a different sphere of influence. Whatever you are called to do, know this: you will face challenges, but you will overcome if you don't quit.

Your area of influence is where your strength will come. That territory is where you will soar like an eagle so that you can accomplish the assignment. Since God has the blueprints for your life mapped out, don't you think He can get you there and provide for you along the way?

It isn't the hindrances or setbacks that keep us from fulfilling the things God has for us, it's the way we react to them. It may seem impossible to turn that business around, to get that college degree, or coach the sports team into success, even though you believe it is a great opportunity that God has opened for you. When you focus on giving God the glory for your life and leave the results up to Him, He will come into the situation.

Trust Him to take care of it. He is right there.

You were sent to the earth to accomplish an assignment. This isn't something that has to be decided by a popularity vote or a committee. True, wisdom and guidance are necessary when starting a new project and moving out in ministry requires accountability. Getting counsel about life decisions from people you are close to is important, but many people get upset because they didn't get the approval they were hoping for and give up.

The passion you have for God and the determination to do what He has sent you on this earth to do will be the fuel to move you forward. Position yourself to hear from God and spend time in

His presence. Then get into His Word to get the road map for the path He has for you. I know this sounds elementary, but these are the keys to your victory.

The pressure of the attack is there to bring fear, division, and ultimately defeat, but don't give in. You have more influence than you think and people are depending on you to finish your race. Your assignment is important.

DON'T LET PRIDE GET IN THE WAY

Pride can be a big distraction for those with a divine assignment. The following words can all be used to describe someone who has a high opinion of themselves: [1]

- Arrogant
- Conceited
- Haughty
- Proud
- Self-respecting
- Self-satisfied
- Smug
- Supercilious
- Vain

Pride is an important factor because it reflects the heart and is something God will resist. Pride is what caused Satan to get kicked out of Heaven. The theme of pride is like this little tune, "Me....it's all about me...." No, it's really about the Kingdom of God. That's why when we lose our life, we will find it. It's not about what we want, but about being concerned what God wants and leaving the results up to Him. We don't live out of a desire for accolades or people pleasing, but out of a burning passion to please God and to help others.

PEOPLE PLEASING

Another subtle distraction that can lure us away from our path is trying to make everyone happy. Sometimes it just seems easier to compromise and make everyone happy. It is foolish to think we can make everyone happy because guess what—we won't! Someone is going to get upset in the juggling act of people pleasing. It is better to obey God than sacrifice and just go along with things. Going along with everyone else will only cause more trouble in the end. While going against the grain may result in conflict, doing something against the will of God is worse.

As we pursue God's will and stay laser-focused on the assignment He gives us, many lives will be restored, families will celebrate life, and regions around the city will be affected and brought to reformation. The steadfast love of the Lord will be shown to His covenant people, whom He has chosen for His purposes. Don't give up. Don't quit.

PRAYER

Father,

Thank You for choosing me for an assignment and for the gifts You have given me to accomplish that assignment. Help me to do what is pleasing to You and not be concerned with what others think. Please give me wise mentors to be accountable to, and I will be careful to obey You. I want to follow Your instructions and not just do what everyone else is doing. Help me hear Your voice, Father.

Please help me guard my heart, and to have pure motives for my service to the Kingdom of God. I want to be in right-standing with You and not do things just for eye-service. Thank You for helping me have courage to keep my focus on You and be strong. Amen.

CHAPTER 4

Jesus is Calling

Listen to His Voice

There is a sound in the earth. Jesus is calling His people to show forth His glory. He is preparing His bride for His glorious appearing. Do you hear His voice calling you? He is preparing His people to move in uniform under His command with one spirit, one purpose and one voice. A people who have their eyes fixed on their Savior. They are fearless and relentless with a passion to pursue Jesus.

There is a story in the Bible about when David returns home to Ziklag and finds his camp had been raided, burned, and the women and children taken captive. The Bible says he and the people weep until their strength is gone.[1]

I can imagine his utter discouragement. He also hears that the people are discussing stoning him. The anguish and embitterment of the people is a great burden to David, but he encourages himself in the Lord.

I want to think a moment on this scripture. Have you ever felt so defeated and discouraged you wept until you had no more strength? Have you gone through a season where you have one problem after another one rise up? The first thing David does is to encourage himself. He doesn't wait for someone else to encourage him. I'm sure he reminded himself of all the victories God has given him before. Sometimes there isn't anyone else around, and you have to be your own encourager. I imagine he meditated on how God had been with him, and the victories he walked out because of God's divine intervention. He might have sung some psalms and worshipped God.

Whatever situation you may find yourself in today, the two words that come to my mind are "encourage yourself." Don't wait for someone else to come along to encourage you. After he encouraged himself, David inquired of the Lord. He prayed and asked the Lord if he should go up against these people who brought this destruction and took their wives and children, and whether he would get the victory.

A very important principal here is to inquire of the Lord. Sometimes the answer can be obvious, or it may be hidden, but it is always important to get the instructions from the Lord. The anointing is in the instructions.

The instinct many times may be to get into fear and take the matter into our own hands to work through the problem. Fear is a trap the enemy uses to discourage us and get our eyes on the problem. David encouraged himself in the Lord. He used a devastating circumstance and remembered how God had delivered him before.

DIVINE INTERVENTION

God answers David, and His instructions were, "Pursue for you will certainly overtake them, and you will certainly rescue the captives."[2] David gathers six hundred men and begins the journey toward the enemy. However, once they reach a brook to get some water, some of the men cannot continue pursuing the enemy because they are too exhausted. David moves forward and continues with the men, determined to get their wives and children back. Just like David, keep pressing forward with those who are moving forward—never go back or allow others to hold you back.

As they pursue the Amalekites, some of the men find an Egyptian in the field. He had been without water and food and is extremely weak. The men want to find out more about this man they'd found and give him some food and water. When his strength returns, he begins telling them where he is from and all about the attack on Ziklag.

The Egyptian tells him he is a servant from Egypt and had not eaten for three days and nights because his master abandoned him after he became sick. He then begins telling David and his men how the Amalekites burned the city of Ziklag and took the women and children captive.

David asks the Egyptian where the Amalekite camp is and asks him to take him and his men there. The servant fears David will hand him over to his master, so he asks David to swear he won't hand him over, and then agrees to take David and his men there. So, David agrees. This is an amazing story about how God leads David and these four hundred men right to this Egyptian servant, who knows exactly where their wives and children are.

Are there people crossing your path God has divinely placed to bring you to your miracle? Stir up the faith inside of you and get the revelation God can bring people across your path in a way that may seem like a coincidence. However, God is not in the coincidence business. He can divinely set you up for a miracle. He knows your address, your thoughts, and can even put a thought in your mind to take another route home instead of the usual route. He can bring a person to your mind to call or arrange circumstances to delay you when traveling. Just like God brought David's men to the Egyptian servant, He can bring you to a divine appointment.

GREAT VICTORY

The Bible says in that passage David recovers all, including the two wives taken captive. David is so glad to be back with his wives and possessions, he doesn't think anything at all about giving the men who stayed behind what is theirs. However, the men who fought the Amalekites with David are angry when David wants to give the men who stayed behind their possessions. They don't mind David giving them their wives, but the other possessions are off limits. After all, they didn't go and find the enemy. They were too exhausted while getting a drink at the brook and had to go back home.

Listen to what David tells the men in 1 Samuel 30:23:

> "You must not do that with what the Lord has given us. He protected us and delivered into our hands the raiding party who came against us. Who will listen to what you say? The share of the man who stayed with the supplies is to be the same as that of him who went down to the battle. All will share alike."

David doesn't act in pride and elevate himself because of his deed or place more value on himself for what he has done. He honors those who went to battle and those who protected the supplies. He shows gratitude to God by staying humble instead of bringing attention to himself. I believe this attitude is why God brought such great victory. He not only gives to the men in his camp, but also to surrounding regions where he and his men had been.

God resists the proud but gives grace to the humble.[3] I believe because David is bringing glory to God in this situation and not himself, it opens the door for God to bless him. It is so important to David he makes it an ordinance and statute which stand to this day.

As a teenager, David spent many years tending to his father's sheep and worshiped God while out in the fields. He drew close to God for protection for himself and the sheep from wolves and lions. He had an intimate relationship with the Lord and felt His presence. He knew the still small voice giving him instruction, comfort, and peace. The same applies to you. Jesus is calling you to draw near to Him and join Him in His work in the earth. He desires us to walk in a deeper relationship with Him and wants to bring a revelation of His love. He said that apart from Him we can do nothing.[4]

WASH, RINSE, REPEAT

You can't keep doing the same thing and expect different results. God wants to break the patterns and habits from your previous season in life that have caused defeat. Is fear of failure going to hold you back? Are you going to expect defeat? Prepare to receive the answer. The most important thing you can do is love God and everyone else. Let God be glorified in everything you do. Do you sometimes give up too soon when you could go further? He will never give up on you, my friend. You are not alone.

Keep your heart focused on God and not your circumstances. When you receive the answer, praise Him, but even if you don't receive when or how you thought you should, praise Him. Praise Him because of who He is. God will take what the enemy planned for destruction and turn it around to His glory for good.

The answer is on the way. In God's Word He says, "Do not fear" 365 times. God can help you do the impossible. So, don't solely look at your own ability. Miracles occur when God has His way, and all will see how great He is.

PRAYER

Father,

Thank You for helping me to encourage myself when I feel discouraged. I know You are with me and have not left me alone. Help me know what to do and how to understand Your instructions. I know the anointing is in the instructions. I will draw near to You in prayer and worship.

I will stay humble and give the glory to You when I receive your answer. Give me eyes to see and recognize Your divine intervention. Thank You for giving me strength to pursue Your promises. I will not accept defeat, and I will not fear. I will prepare to receive Your answer and keep my heart focused on You. Amen.

CHAPTER 5
Like Jewels in a Crown

Be a Bridge to the Next Generation

A family is designed by God to carry strength and strategic purpose for the Kingdom of God and to leave a legacy. God so desires for families to be built on love for God and for each other. One practical way to build strength and unity in the family is to consider the bigger picture and see each person's strengths, abilities, and talents. A positive and contagious style of living will develop with this type of lifestyle and help keep the focus on the future goals, not on the present conflicts that might exist.

Not every family has two parents living in the home together, so each parent's example of commitment to God by living out what is expected of the children is key. The children can only imitate what they see. Once children reach their toddler and preschool years, they are well on their way to developing their personality.

Moving everyone in the family in the same direction gets a little more challenging if everyone is going their own way.

STRATEGIC PURPOSE

Having a family vision and maintaining standards is a key to building the relationships that keep everyone on track. Some examples of family standards are:

1. Knowing God and agreeing with His Word.
2. Treating others with respect and kindness.
3. Saying "I'm sorry" and asking for forgiveness.
4. Seeking God for His will and purpose.

As the children watch a parent model the way they are supposed to act, think, and live, it makes it easier to navigate the entire tribe that direction. When God wants the parent to seek Him for direction, it is a great opportunity to set aside special time to teach the children about praying to find answers from God. The children can learn about forgiveness and telling God they are sorry when they have done something wrong. The children can begin to learn about refraining for a short time from things they really want to do such as when an adult will fast to teach them about self-control. They can refrain from things like watching television, eating candy or dessert, or playing with one of their favorite toys or video games.

It's in these daily choices a family lays a foundation for the vision of the family. It doesn't matter if there is one child or fourteen children, the same principles apply. The children will grow up understanding more about having a relationship with God, with each other and how to be responsible for their actions. There are so many life lessons learned when the foundation at home is established.

RAISING GODLY CHILDREN IN AN UNGODLY WORLD

Having children is a gift from God. Children are like arrows to be sent out with purpose, carrying on their destiny for the Kingdom of God. When my children were growing up in our home, we would have devotions as a family several nights during the week. We would read out of the children's books and then graduated to youth devotionals when they got older. They learned scripture memory at a very early age and discovered there are consequences for disobedience.

The principles God had us teach our children were principles He requires His children to live by. We wanted our children to know God for themselves and trained them to hear God with a relationship through Christ. The Word of God demonstrates those in book after book, both in the Old and New Testament. Teaching with this method made it easy for our children to grasp what the Bible says and how God thinks. It also helped them to be more fruitful in the ultimate dedication of their lives to the Lord.

Laying the foundation early on is a key to victory with raising Godly children:

> "Therefore, everyone who hears these words of Mine, and acts on them, may be compared to a wise man, who built his house on the rock. And

the rain fell, and the floods came, and the winds blew and slammed against that house; and yet it did not fall, for it had been founded on the rock."[1]

Making the Word of God the standard for living is something a child will keep in his or her heart, even into adulthood. The Word of God will be in their heart because they are taught to live by it. It is a standard the world can't easily change. The principles in the Word reinforce the "why" and the "how" of instruction in the day-to-day raising of the child and give the child a plumb line to go by as they get older. If this isn't in place when they are young, the risk is they will mold to their environment or to peer pressure.

Being a parent isn't to be taken lightly. There is a great responsibility to demonstrate and model the behavior we want our children to walk in. They will only parrot what they see and hear. This lifestyle will hold them accountable to God as they get older. The struggle during the teenage years will be reduced if not absent with the Word of God as their standard. They will know the reverence of God and the "fear" of God.

THE REWARD IS IN THE FRUIT

The ultimate reward for a parent is to see their child grow up and live with Christian values. One of the most important lessons a child can learn is to find purpose in their life as a child of God. Many adults live their lives never knowing why they are on this earth.

One easy way to teach the children about purpose is to get them involved in extracurricular activities. Having a child in sports, for example, can be a very busy time, both in the child's and parent's season of life. There are the practices, then the games—then more practices. It is an endless cycle of hurry up and wait. A goal to build character is to help the child carry his or her purpose and vision beyond just winning the game. The focus should be on developing character and integrity through the practice and the game. It isn't enough just to win.

As small people in training, children must learn the importance of looking after others and not just focusing on themselves. The thrust of the vision is to put God's principles and commandments first, and to treat others the way they want to be treated. I believe God does command parents to build that character in children, so when they are grown they will not turn from it.

LEAVING A LEGACY

When a parent verbally blesses their child, it causes the child to feel value. Children need to feel loved by their parents. Jesus was gentle with children and offered loving affirmation. Jesus was also gentle when He spoke to children and not harsh or condemning. When a parent uses their God-given authority to encourage and affirm their children it inspires them toward future success, helps them feel valued and gives them vision for their future. It's an investment into a child that can positively shape their self-image.

An example of blessing the child is pointing out a child's skill, character or strength. Saying things like, "I think others appreciate you because...," or "You're really good at...," or "You're so thoughtful when you..." affirms the child can do something well and encourages them to strive for excellence. This also celebrates and inspires the child's uniqueness and individuality.

Your children will begin to absorb your words into their hearts, be influenced about who they pick for friends, and develop a healthy standard for their own lives. When they are around people who encourage them, they are influenced by the actions they see and the words they hear. Parents who are true to their word and follow through with what they say, whether it is a promise to spend time with the child or correction to bad behavior, will reinforce the authority they have with their child. It lets the child know they can trust the parent and sets an example of faithfulness.

Another important attribute for children's character is the fear of the Lord. So many parents are afraid their children won't love them if they hold their child accountable from their actions. Suffering consequences for our actions is a very real-life lesson and children need to understand it. If they don't learn it when they are under your care, they will learn it from the judicial system when they are an adult.

This lifestyle is a focus on the Kingdom of God, not entitlement. It focuses on what is right, even when they don't see others doing it. It focuses on truth, even when others are deceitful. It focuses on faithfulness and does not excuse a person who quits or becomes complacent.

Going to church together and worshipping as a family teaches your children not only by example about worshipping God but also builds a stronger family by laying a foundation for their lifestyle.

These principles are found in Deuteronomy 6:1-19. Teach your children to hide the Word of God in their heart and live it out before your children. Give your children an example of what Christ looks and acts like, and they will walk humbly before their God. God promises in His Word to bless the family who does these things, to a thousand generations.

PRAYER

Father,

Thank You for my children. They are a gift from You, and I am so thankful. Please help me to demonstrate how to live a righteous life, and how to live by Your Word. Help me to follow Your commandments and teach my children to as well. I want to speak blessings over my children and take time for them. Help me to be a good influence and help them feel loved by my words.

I pray my children will follow You all the days of their life and never turn from You. May I see the reward of this fruit in my children's lives as I train them in Your Word and instruct them to follow Your commandments—to a thousand generations. Amen

CHAPTER 6

Quitting is Not an Option

Follow the Road Map for Your Life

Have you experienced a season where life threw you a curve ball? Maybe a storm came along, and you were not prepared for it? Has there been a dream in your heart you have prayed for that looks like it will never happen? Let me share a story with you that I believe will encourage you.

A family I know had been faithful in helping others with personal projects and giving of their time and resources. Their children are also very compassionate and self-sacrificing. This family loves to be a blessing to others. While they were out eating dinner, a fire broke out in their home and destroyed everything.

This family didn't want to ask for help but they didn't have much savings left because they had to use it to live on. One day, a person who knew the family was talking to a mutual friend because they wanted to help the family but didn't have much extra to make a big difference. The mutual friend was greatly moved by this family's tragedy and had the resources to help them. They knew it would mean a lot to the family and their desperate situation.

After receiving the gift, the family was able to rebuild their home and replace some possessions lost in the fire. All the times they sowed into the lives of others came back to them in a big way right when they needed it. They were able to turn this difficult situation into a testimony.

What are you sowing into the lives of others? Do you help people with their projects or give food to the food pantry or a family you hear is in need? Do you stop what you are doing in a store and pray for someone, or offer resources to those who are going through rough times? God sees everything you do, and it doesn't go unnoticed by your Father.

What you pour into others will come back to you. It's law of reaping and sowing. Walk by faith, even when the answer is not seen. Isn't that what the definition of faith really is? The Bible says without faith it is impossible to please God.1 This precious family could have focused on the negative and most likely would not have seen their miracle. Instead of living in fear and talking about how bad it was, they decided to put their trust in God's ability to help them and God restored their home to them. They were focused on all God's Word says about His help in time of need and remembered how He had come to their rescue before. They rehearsed past victories, and it gave them faith to trust God in their rough season.

JOY OF THE LORD IS YOUR STRENGTH

How's the joy factor in your life? There is a real spiritual force that pushes the momentum of our circumstances forward when joy is the factor and the purpose of our thoughts. As a man thinks in his heart, so is he.[2] Joy is not necessarily an inner feeling of happiness, but the result of a decision to have the right attitude and do the right thing. As we press into the promises God has given us, we hold them fast in our hearts and use the eyes of faith to see the answer before it manifests. This releases hope and joy in our hearts though the answer is unseen in the natural.

It's a choice. We either stare at the problem, sickness, or offense and listen to the hopeless words coming into our mind or believe God's promise. I'm sure you've heard the lies – "You'll never get out of debt... You can't get healed from that disease... Your marriage will never get better." The other choice is to believe God's Word and know that His promises are sure.

One of the ways to let joy fill our heart is to start praising God. I like to turn on worship music and feel the comfort of His presence. It's in His presence we experience the fullness of His joy.

As we turn out hearts and mind to Jesus and stay laser-focused on Him, everything around us gets in alignment with His will and His Word, and we can then gain a perspective on our circumstances. It is then we can see the opportunities opening before us, and it brings clarity when we hear His voice. Our lives are like a puzzle God is putting together, with one piece at a time. If a piece is missing, He knows how to work that piece into our lives as an opportunity. If a piece gets broken, God is faithful, and we can trust Him to restore it.

God will work everything in our lives together for good. He is the God of the turn-around. He is God of the impossible. When it looks like there is no way, He will make a way. He will open doors that no man can close, and close doors that no man can open.

He is not a cookie-cutter God, and He can do anything He wants, anyway He wants. So, be open to opportunities as you seek His face, and be willing to try something new. Remember, God is a creative God, and there is no searching His understanding. Just look at all the crawling creatures and how different they are. The flowers all have different shapes, colors, and characteristics. If the flowers in the field are beautiful and unique, how much more can your God who created the universe create a way for you!

WHO ARE YOU TAKING TO YOUR FUTURE?

In some seasons, God will bring people into our lives, and in other seasons, He will remove them. He has the big picture in mind for our lives and sees how we are fitly joined together to bring about His will. However, we have the will and choice to move forward without people who are not aligning with the vision God has placed in our heart.

Have you had someone in your life constantly speak negatively about your ideas? Are there moments you feel discouraged about your circumstances if a certain person is in your company? If you answered "yes" to these questions, this may be the season God is opening your eyes to make choices about who you are taking with you into your future, and who you may need to move on without.

To take hold of the new you must let go of the old. You cannot drive in forward gear if you are always looking back in your review mirror. Sometimes this can include people in our lives. To whom much is given much is required.[3] God has called His people to a standard the world does not understand. We cannot please the world and God at the same time. In the kingdom of God, there is no room for compromise in the Kingdom of God.

You must press toward to mark of the high calling and forget those things which are behind to obtain the prize.[4] You may not be where you want to be, but you are not where we used to be—and the best is still to come. God wants to bring you to a new page and start a new chapter in your life to accomplish the things He has planned for you. His destiny for you is far greater than the temporary things seen with the natural eye.

HOPE FOR TODAY

There is a hope tucked deep in our spirit that no man can take away—the hope we can cling to in the promises of God. Let's go a little deeper on this subject. When our family was looking for the land to build our house, I had prayed and prayed, asking God to reveal where this land was. The land I wanted to buy just didn't seem possible. We had looked at two different properties we loved, but we couldn't close on them for one reason or another.

Almost every property we looked at seemed like a dead-end. As I was praying about it one morning, I laid it down and asked God to reveal our new property location to my husband. Literally that weekend, my husband went to a very small rural town to work and came back with an amazing revelation: he had found our location. Because it was a rural area, it was hard to find a realtor. I called the nearest town's real estate firm and asked for their help. A kind lady answered the phone, and after describing all the details of what I wanted, she very reluctantly told me she would check into it. She just happened to know a relator in that area but was honest in telling me she wasn't sure she could find what I was looking for in my price range.

In five minutes, she called me back and excitedly told me about a property that had literally come back on the market the day before and was not much higher than my price range. She told me the only problem was that it had about seven more acres than I had asked for. My family drove up to the property to meet her, and it was exactly as I had asked for in detail—down to the white fence and bushes with pink flowers. It was beautiful, and we purchased our land in only four weeks.

Our dream home was now becoming a reality, and we were seeing the hand of God move circumstances to get us into that area. Our hope was birthed in His promises of provision, and we knew He was going to do what He said. Is there a dream you are praying for? Have you had roadblocks to your quest for His will, only to find yourself at a dead-end? Keep pressing forward, holding fast to His promises, and the Father will reveal

His direction to you. He loves to show Himself mighty on our behalf and reveal His power.

NO GIANT IS TOO BIG

What giant are you facing right now? Is it a job loss or financial setback? Are you going through marital problems? Are you grieving from the loss of a loved one? Is it a health challenge or a business stuck in neutral? God can give you the secret to your breakthrough. God will remember you and give you the wisdom to accomplish your goals. I want to encourage you to keep your face like flint towards Jesus and focus on His Word. The trial isn't too big for God, and He will remember you if you stay focused on Him.

You could be on the brink of your breakthrough when you turn this corner. Many times, right before a breakthrough, there is a battle, hindrance, or setback. God will give you the favor to accomplish your dreams. He knows the promises you are holding onto and has already made a way for you. He wants to reveal how to tap into His provision, healing, and restoration. He put those dreams in your heart and will bring revelation for you to accomplish them. Always know you will never accomplish your dreams if you quit–quitting is not an option.

PRAYER

Father,

Thank You for helping me to help others around me and be a resource of strength. I know You will be faithful to see what I do and help me in my time of need. Help me turn my heart and mind to Jesus and stay laser-focused on You. I will watch my attitude and praise You for who You are. I ask You to show me any relationships I have that need to change. Bring revelation of the people You are taking with me to my future and those You are not.

Help me to see the opportunities You bring across my path, to stay in faith and keep dreaming. No giant is too big for You. Father, please reveal the secret to my breakthrough. Thank You for giving me strength and to pursue Your promises. I will not quit but will fulfill the dreams and passions You have put in my heart. Amen.

CHAPTER 7
Health and Happiness

Today, I Choose Joy

Health can be measured not only physically but also spiritually. I pray that all is well with you and that your body is as healthy as I know your soul is.[1] But perhaps you are having some of these symptoms of ill spiritual health that mimic physical ailments?

1. Low temperature—Lukewarm.
2. Heart problems—Cold, indifferent, and without love.
3. Loss of appetite—Not hungry for spiritual food.
4. Difficulty breathing—A "duty" to pray.
5. Lethargy—Unwilling to serve, non-giving.
6. Craving for unhealthy things—"Lover of themselves, lovers of money, boastful, proud, abusive, disobedient to their parents, ungrateful, unholy, without love, unforgiving, slanderous, without self-control, brutal, not

lovers of the good, treacherous, rash, conceited, lover of pleasure rather than lovers of God—having a form of godliness but denying its power. Have nothing to do with such people."[2]

STEPS TO HEALING:

1. Loss of appetite—Listen to the gospel preached and study the Word of God daily. The appetite will improve.
2. Heart problems—Forgive: "For if you forgive other people when they sin against you, your heavenly Father will also forgive you. But if you do not forgive others their sins, your Father will not forgive your sins."[3]
3. Difficulty breathing—Do not restrain prayer. Pray without ceasing.
4. Lethargy—Exercise yourself unto fruitfulness. He told them, 'The harvest is plentiful, but the workers are few. Ask the Lord of the harvest, therefore, to send out workers into His harvest field.'"[4]
5. Craving unhealthy things—Love the Lord your God with all your heart, mind and strength. Breathe the atmosphere of Calvary.

AS YOUR SOUL PROSPERS

"The more objects you set your heart upon, the more thorns there are to tear your peace of mind to shreds."[5] The body is the temple of the Lord, and it is vital to take care of it. Good health is important to living a long life. However, there is more to health than just eating well. Exercise and having positive mental health, a healthy self-image and a healthy lifestyle are also important.

What about your soul? What does it mean for your soul to prosper? The soul is made up of three-parts: the mind, will, and emotions. Your soul is the very essence of who you are. It is the core of your being. God does not control your soul. If He did, He would violate your free-will choice. For your soul to prosper, there are some principles I would like to share with you.

The first principle is to have the mind of Christ. "Do not conform to the pattern of this world but be transformed by the renewing of your mind. Then you will be able to test and approve what God's will is—his good, pleasing and perfect will."[6] Your mind will begin to prosper as you renew your mind to Christ's and His Word.

The second principle follows naturally after the first, and that is your will. Once you begin to renew your mind to the mind of Christ, your choices and actions will begin to conform to those thoughts. As you begin to circumcise your heart and rid your mind and will of things that are unhealthy, the cravings of your soul will draw you toward pure and fruitful desires and habits. "Above all else, guard your heart. For everything you do flows from it."[7]

The third principle is emotions. Interestingly, our emotions actually start with thoughts. The emotions are associated with the five senses—taste, smell, see, hear and touch. Our emotions are always related to at least one of the five senses.

Our thoughts and emotions need to be lined up with the Word of God. If they aren't we won't demonstrate self-control, and things can get out of control. How big is your sack of emotional pain? We all carry emotional baggage to varying degrees of painful memories. It might be grief over the loss of a loved one, loss of a job, the devastating break-up of a marriage, or the trauma of physical illness. Lack of trust can result from suffering rejection, betrayal, or shame, as well as various trials and hardship, guilt, loss of self-esteem, or sorrow.

It takes a lot more energy to store pain than to confront it. Studies have shown that negative emotions can weaken your body, while positive emotions can strengthen your body. Shame has devastating effects and is usually followed by guilt, apathy, grief, fear, anxiety, anger and hate.[8]

Research shows that fear triggers more than 1,400 known physical and chemical responses and activates more than 30 different hormones. There are medical reasons to forgive. Toxic waste generated by toxic thoughts can cause diseases like diabetes, cancer, asthma, skin problems, and allergies to name a few. Anger toward another person is just as deadly as ingesting poison. Negative emotions can inhibit your ability to have joy and can cause you to settle for less than your soul needs to flourish.[9]

HAPPINESS VS. JOY

"I perceived that there is nothing better for them than to be joyful and to do good as long as they live; also, that everyone should eat and drink and take pleasure in all his toil—this is God's gift to man."[10] Everyone wants to be happy, healthy, and prosperous and to enjoy everyday living. Let me ask you a question: what would you need in your life to be happy? I know when different responsibilities in my life begin to crowd my day, I begin to analyze if I really need to be doing that project, or if I can arrange my daily schedule so I have more time to relax.

One thing that can wear us down is having a day full of things to do that aren't bearing fruit. When I start feeling drained of energy, I will take an inventory of my projects to see if I need to change my day or eliminate something. Being too busy will take away the joy.

So many times, people are inclined to say they will be happy based on what needs to happen in their lives to gain fulfillment. The emphasis is placed on defining when an event takes place for the happiness to occur. What would happen if the focus was on God's plan for our life and not on the everyday results?

"People are basically the same the world over. Everybody wants the same things—to be happy, to be healthy, to be at least reasonably prosperous, and to be secure. They want friends, peace of mind, good family relationships, and hope that tomorrow is going to be even better than today."[11]

HEALTH AND WELLNESS

One of the greatest concerns as we get older is our health. Many people are searching the internet for self-help remedies, alternative health, and nutritional information. As I realized the baby boomers are the next aging generation, I began recognizing the health trends with this generation. I discovered more and more baby boomers as they reach retirement age are turning to alternative health practitioners as a resource for the treatment and daily nutritional guides.

These alternative health practitioners, or holistic doctors, include practices for chiropractic care, acupuncture, massage therapy, personal trainers, and nutritionists, to name a few. In my quest for answers, I found many of the boomers are caring for their aging parents in their homes, and most likely will follow the same pattern of staying in their home to be cared for. Who wouldn't want to stay in their home and thrive in their elder years?

The passion to help people find healing in more natural substances is what lead me to start my business, Mountain Top Health and Wellness. I truly believe we are moving toward healthcare trends where people opt for alternative treatment whenever possible to maintain health. God has already placed healing herbs, foods, and the wisdom to bring healing with what is already in the earth, as is written in Revelation 22:1-2:

> "The angel showed me the river of the water of life, as clear as crystal, flowing from the throne of God and of the Lamb down the middle of the street of the city. On each side of the river stood the tree of life, bearing twelve crops of fruit, yielding every month. And the leaves of the tree are for the healing of the nations."

God is giving us a glimpse into how to be healed by eating the right foods and drinking water. The leaves of the trees are extracts and roots we now have on this earth.

The herbs myrrh, aloe, and frankincense, to name a few, are mentioned in the Bible and illustrate God's health plan for us. The more we care for our bodies with natural and organic foods, the better our lives will be both inside and out.

Medical doctors are remarkable at caring for people, and I am sure God gave these precious people the ability to perform miracles through medicine. Let's not move away from traditional medicine but embrace God's plan for our health with the pathway to healing He has provided.

Discover how to prosper in health through alternative wellness by visiting my website at www.mthealthandwellness.com.

PRAYER

Father,

Thank You for the truth of Your Word. I hunger and thirst for Your truth and for the refreshing of Your Word. Renew my mind as I read and meditate on Your holy Word. Let revelation come to me as I seek Your ways and conform to Your will.

Give me wisdom to know if alternative health is Your pathway to my healing. Show me Your ways to health and healing. Please help me run my race to the fullest without my life being cut short by disease. I want to receive peace in my mind, confidence in my spirit, and health for my body. I will keep pressing forward and hold fast to Your promises as I wait on You to reveal Your direction for me. Thank you for showing me Your power and might on my behalf. Amen.

CHAPTER 8
Staying in the Game

Calm and Laser-Focused

Once I was watching a movie with a story about a high school football game. The team is losing by a wide margin, and it doesn't look like the losing team has a chance. The opposing team seems to be more skilled—they have more variety of plays and are faster. They are putting scores on the board, one play right after the other.

The coach tries to come up with new plays and gives the team a quick pep-talk in their time-outs, but the opposing team appears to have the upper hand. They score a touchdown, then turn around, intercept the ball, and take off down the field to score another touchdown. Finally, when the game is over, the losing team stares at the scoreboard and listens to the crowd roar with applause and cheers for their opponent's victory.

Exhausted, frustrated, and discouraged, the team meets back in the locker room with the coaches after the game. The greeting by the head coach is encouraging as he tells the team how proud he is of them, and how impressed he is at their strength and ability to persevere to the end.

As they look at their coach to embrace his words of wisdom, hope begins to emerge in their hearts and shine from their faces. He tells them he is glad to be their coach, and they don't have anything to be ashamed of because they did their best. As they kneel in prayer to close out the night, the coach listens to one of the students as he leads the team in prayer and is greatly moved. The student prays, "We will praise you when we win, and we will praise you when we lose. We praise you for who you are." This team has had a losing streak for six years. They have to overcome a bad mindset, bad habits formed, and a bad reputation.

For the first time in six years, they start winning because they changed their mindset. The game they are playing is no longer about them, but about the standard they live by. It is about their relationship with God and with each other. They have learned a new way of thinking, new habits and began praising God and honoring God with their lives—this new concept of living is what gives them the momentum to keep going, even during what appears to be defeat.

The next scene shows the assistant coaches putting up the uniforms and discussing the year's progress for the team. Suddenly, in walks the head coach, and he is told by one of the assistant coaches about a previous phone message. The next scene shows the head coach calling a team meeting and informs them they will be playing the next game in the playoffs because the team they just lost to was disqualified.

The team is excited, to say the least, and wins that next game in the playoffs. We will call this team, "Team A." This twist in events sets the stage for the next game against a team who had taken the trophy for first place over the last few years. This team is very big, very strong, and numerous in size. It is time for them to face their giants. We will call this team "Team B."

As Team A plays their game to the best of their ability, it is down to the last few minutes in the fourth quarter. Team A intercepts the ball and runs to the 40-yard line. The game is so close at the end of the game, and Team A needs this field goal to win. They don't have enough time to run down the field for a touchdown and don't want to risk getting tackled.

To add to the plot, the farthest distance their kicker had made during the season was 35-yards. The Team A student is in a tough spot, and the win is resting on him. He needs to choose between doing his best and leaving the results up to God, or caving into the pressure and giving up.

The teams line up, and the kicker for Team A kicks the ball right as the wind direction changes. The wind carries the ball, and it goes right through the middle of the field goal. The timer runs out, and the game is over. The crowd roars with cheers and excitement as the Team A wins the state championship.

This small team (Team A) beats a large team twice their size and strength and takes the state championship away from a team who had carried that title for several years. They faced their giants and won. They praised God and honored Him with their lives.[1]

Don't let past failures keep you in the mindset of defeat. Allow your life to honor God, face your giants of defeat, fear and failure, and praise Him for who He is. God can turn the tide when you face the giants. Stay strong, persevere, and be determined to stay in the game to receive your victory.

YOU ARE GOD'S LEADER

Sometimes the enemy will whisper in our ears words of inadequacy or discouragement because of circumstances. He tempts us with the lust of the flesh, lust of the eyes, and the pride of life. His lies attempt to permeate our mind with the illusion that it's good not to try harder—just compromise with mediocrity. His deceitful, subtle distortions tell us not to help another person because someone else will take care of it.

The Lord wants to shed some light on your path and get you to the end-zone. The assignment set before you may seem like it's impossible. You might feel like it's too late in the game of life because it's the "fourth quarter" and the finish line is far away.

Jesus is our example, and He showed us how to persevere in the wilderness while the enemy is tempting us. He taught us in the Word to speak to the storm to calm the waves. The leadership in you must shine, especially during the storm. Jesus told us this, "In this world you will have trouble. But take heart! I have overcome the world."[2]

Yes, you are tired and weary, and you don't know how many more steps you can take. I want to encourage you today—you can get to the finish line, my friend. So many people are counting on you and need your leadership. The problem is contagious, and if you start to give up, it will show those around you it's okay for them to give up.

Many Christians are hungry to understand how to walk out their victory and need an example. Those who have understanding and knowledge of the Word are positioned to be the example of Jesus to them. Will you say "yes" to Jesus, and be that example?

IT'S TIME FOR YOUR COMEBACK

You may not be where you want to be in your future, but you are not where you used to be. Your best is yet to come. It's your comeback time, my friend. Is there a mindset from your past experiences—a giant you are facing in your life? You are not defined by your past experiences, but they will prepare you for your future if you allow them to.

Let Isaiah 61:3 remind you that God will give you beauty for ashes and joy for mourning. Allow the adversities of your past to stretch you and grow you into greater confidence. God wants to bring something good from the negative in your life. He promises to bring beauty for ashes and joy for mourning.

A palm tree is a good example of bouncing back after a bad storm. The palm tree is designed to bend but not break during high winds. Palm trees may be bent over four to five hours but will not break. They bounce back.

Palm trees have strong roots that go deep into the earth. During times of high wind, the palm tree is bent over, but the root system of the tree goes deeper into the earth. The high winds strengthen the tree, and this gives it opportunities for growth. The wind calms down, and the palm tree bounces back in an upright position.

It's your time to bounce back and allow the experiences you are going through to strengthen you. Put your faith and trust in God to turn your situation around and cause you to flourish like a palm tree. When you are tempted to give up on your dreams because of the high winds blowing all around you, remember, you are the seed of the Almighty God. The same power that raised Jesus Christ from the dead lives in you. No challenge or storm is too difficult for you.

Don't just settle for mediocrity, sickness, or defeat. Rise-up and declare your faith in God. Recognize your victory comes from God, and He is on your side. He will show himself mighty on your behalf if you don't give up.

PRAYER

Father,

Thank You for turning the tide in my life. I will not let past failures keep me in the mindset of defeat. I will stay strong, persevere, and be determined to stay in the game to receive my victory. Even though I am tired and weary, I will persevere because I know people are counting on me. I want to be an example to others. I want the leader in me to shine a light on their path.

Give me strength and faith to trust You in my situation. I declare I am the seed of the Almighty God. The same power that raised Jesus from the dead lives in me. I can do all things through Christ who strengthens me.

I will be like the palm tree and flourish. I know my roots of faith that are in You will go deeper as the winds of change blow. Show Yourself mighty on my behalf. Amen.

CHAPTER 9

The Perfect Balance

Make Today Amazing

Are you wearing several hats and juggling life on a shoestring? How about the mom hat, being a home educator, owning a business, or working full-time? Do you find it challenging to serve your husband well after a full day of "other daily activities" and feel you are being stretched too thin?

You are not alone, my friend. Many people, especially women, find it difficult to get everything done and feel energetic by the end of the day. Time management is an ongoing challenge, and yet we all need to master it. I want you to grab your cup of coffee or tea, find a comfortable spot, and relax. I have some refreshing news to share with you.

I first want to thank you for listening. Listening is a skill that helps leaders take their place of influence to another level.

Secondly, I want to tell you how appreciated you are. Without your commitment and dedication to your family and work or ministry, there would be a great void.

You have talents and gifts to be used, and there isn't another person on this earth to do what you are called to do. Your gifts and callings are unique and much appreciated. You may be asking what gifts and talents can it take to be a homemaker or work as a receptionist? It takes the gifts residing within you, and you are equipped to do exactly what you are doing. Many times, as moms and wives, it may not seem like a big task to complete our daily routines. However, it is so important, and that is why God set you in that family for you to take care of everything.

So, I want you to know you are so important to God, He doesn't want you to neglect yourself. You are so valuable to His plans in this earth, and you cannot let yourself be left behind in the hustle and bustle of your everyday world. Yes, I know all must get done, and that is why you must schedule in some "me" time for yourself.

BEAUTY BY DESIGN

You were created beautiful from the inside out, and God wants you to know how special you are to Him. He created you with a unique beauty that nobody else has on this earth. You have certain physical features He created just for you to wear. Don't ever put yourself down, covet another woman's features, or feel inferior to another woman's physical appearance.

The Bible says we are to love our neighbor as we love ourselves. Yes, God wants you to love yourself enough to take care of yourself, enhance your beauty inside and out, and be your best. Beauty is so much more than the adornment of jewels and expensive clothing. Rather, it is the genuine and sweet spirit within a woman that makes her beautiful. Always remember that without love, we are just a resounding gong and a clanging symbol—just making a lot of noise.

Yes, I believe God also wants us to enhance our beauty on the outside, as He does promise to renew our youth. Here are some ideas on taking a break from the usual routine to give yourself some time.

BALANCE FOR YOUR BODY

Balancing your diet is essential in today's world of pollutants and food driven culture. Take a look at the nutritional value in food from the local supermarket:

> "Research shows organic foods have 25% more vitamins, minerals, and phytonutrients because the top soil is better cared for and protected. Organic foods contain higher levels of beta carotene, vitamins C, D, and E, health-promoting polyphenols, cancer-fighting antioxidants, essential fatty acids, and essential minerals."[1]

Today, fruits and vegetables are repeatedly grown on the same land, in soil depleted of nutrients, vitamins, and minerals. When fertilizers are used on the plants, it doesn't support human health, although it helps the plant survive. As a result, humans find toxins in the fruits and vegetables, a cause for many diseases and health concerns.

"Some fertilizers are now considered obesogens—endocrine disruptors that increase risk of obesity. Excessive hormone exposure increases hormone related cancers in humans. 94% of U.S. beef has added hormones. Chemical-free foods decrease toxin related cancers."[2] Your body needs nutrients to fight off the toxins ingested from these pesticides. One way of eliminating the pesticides is to wash your food before preparing it.

Studies have shown that as we age, more nutrients are needed due to malabsorption. Also, as we age, the acidity of our stomach acid becomes more alkaline. Taking digestive enzymes is very helpful, along with taking other natural nutrients.[3] Adding vitamins and minerals to supplement the lack of nutrition in food can bring more immune defense and add vitality to your life. It's important to check with the nutritionist at the health food store in your area where you live to make sure you are getting the best supplement for your needs.

Along with a balanced diet, it is good to establish an exercise routine. Exercise is beneficial for people of any age. There are studies to show how many benefits exercises can bring to a person.[4]

1. It helps keep a person independent as they age.
2. It increases energy.
3. People who exercise have a less risk of diabetes, heart disease, or osteoporosis.

4. It is good for helping with weight control.
5. When strengthening the core, it brings strength and balance to the whole body.
6. Exercise is good for managing stress.

Take some time out of your schedule each week and plan an exercise routine for yourself. Your family will be thankful, and you will feel better physically, emotionally, and mentally.

BALANCE FOR YOUR SOUL

One important factor many people neglect is rest and sleep. Make sure you are getting enough. Simply resting with your eyes closed calms your mind and gives it a break while giving your muscles and organs a rest. Resting and taking a break is so important and can add youthfulness to your life. Getting the right amount of sleep each night is vital to your health. A good's night sleep helps you feel better, brings clarity to your thinking, and keeps your emotions more stable.

Did you know your memory improves with a solid night's sleep? Studies show adults who are learning something new whether physical or mental, your mind retains it better with a good night's sleep.[5] Too much sleep or too little is associated with a shorter life span in adults. Studies have shown more deaths occur in women who get less than five hours of sleep or more than nine hours of sleep a night. Sleep also affects the quality of life.[6, 7]

If you have chronic pain or have had an injury recently, getting enough sleep may help reduce your pain. Many studies have shown the link between sleep loss and lower pain threshold. A good night's sleep can help you with weight control. It leads to an increase in the hormone leptin, which signals being full. Lack of sleep can cause more stress-prone anxiety and will reduce the ability to fight the junk food cravings in the afternoon.[8]

Think about the last time you slept well and woke up feeling optimistic and more energetic. Bad sleep habits can have the opposite effect and make it easier to be cranky, irritable, and less tolerant. Try taking care of a toddler with poor sleep habits—frustration is inevitable. The escape plan here is to get in bed a little earlier. Let your body recharge and restore itself so you can face a busy day tomorrow.

BALANCE FOR YOUR MIND

Studies show that 75% to 90% of illnesses and diseases are a direct result of our thought life. What we think about truly does affect us both physically and emotionally. Did you know our minds and thoughts are either working for us or against us? When it works against us, negative and discouraging thoughts lead to a self-destructive pattern of behavior. Dr. Caroline Leaf, a leading Neuro-Metacognitive learning specialist and committed Christian, notes in her teaching on the brain, "Toxic thinking literally 'wears down' the brain and the rest of the body."[9]

A thought may seem harmless, but thoughts are active and can influence our decisions, words, actions and physical reaction. Our actions can originate from thoughts. A thought can become toxic and become physically, emotionally or spiritually dangerous. Toxic thoughts can trigger negative and anxious emotions, which produce biochemicals that cause the body stress. They are stored in your mind, as well as in the cells of your body.

Your thoughts are like tree branches. As thoughts grow and become permanent, more branches grow and the connections become stronger. This means that you can make an intentional decision to think positively. It will take time for your brain to change the pattern of your mind, but God's grace will take you there, one thought at a time.[10]

Be aware of your thoughts, and your words. You can't say one thing and have your mind think another. It just isn't physically possible. Keeping the mind of Christ and meditating on scriptures is a sure way to keep a positive attitude. Let unforgiveness go. Don't hold onto the argument from yesterday, last week, or ten years ago. It isn't going to do you any good now, anyway. Letting that anger go will release your mind to bring peace to your body, peace to your mind, and give you the peace in your emotions you long for.

BALANCE FOR YOUR TIME

Does it ever feel like there are never enough hours in the day? No matter how you divide it up, there are only 24-hours. Remember one very important lesson: you cannot do it all. If you are a mom trying to juggle the husband, kids, work, ministry, business, and self-care, don't be so hard on yourself.

Try to delegate some basic chores around the house to your kids. Ask the husband to help you with a honey-do list or hire out the cleaning and lawn work if possible. Plan the night before, and make sure you clean up before going to bed. Waking up to a sink full of dishes is only going to bring frustration to your day. So, make sure to have a routine each night to ensure order before going to bed.

Learn to say "no" to outside requests. It can be hard to turn down a friend who needs a favor or a neighbor asking for you to do a quick errand for them. While your intentions may be noteworthy, this little extra act of kindness may cause you to lose time with your family.

You will not get back a single minute, so spending enjoyable time with your family and friends is priceless. You may think your schedule is too tight to fit in a movie or a night out on a date with your husband, but you must learn to appreciate what you have before time forces you to appreciate what you had. Some moms who homeschool may get their lessons ready while their children are eating breakfast. You can throw a load of clothes in the washer while you run errands and multitask to save time during your day if you are a homemaker.

The most important thing to factor in is to be flexible. While it's important to have a routine and keep things organized, unexpected things come up. You can encounter a sick child, the dog that needs to go to the vet, your boss who wants that project completed today or the dinner that gets burned.

Having a rhythm for your day but keeping some backup plans can take out the stress should a hiccup throw you off your schedule. As you wear several hats and journey into your Promise Land, make sure you remember how unique you are and special to God.

Make sure to keep a healthy diet and take good supplements, schedule in some exercise, and get plenty of sleep and rest.

Always keep your mind stayed on Christ and His Word. Let go of any unforgiveness and appreciate the time you have with your family and friends. When you make these choices, and love yourself as you do your neighbor, then you will walk through your life with the perfect balance you long for—one step at a time.

PRAYER

Father,

Thank You for creating me as a unique person. I know You created me with gifts and talents that nobody else has. Reveal to me all that You have for me to do here on Earth. Give me wisdom to know the right diet for me and the supplements I need to be healthy and help me to schedule exercise in my weekly routine.

I want balance in my life, so help me to manage my time better. I want to get the proper sleep and rest so I can be my best and maintain order in my home. Help me rid my thoughts of negativity and discouragement and show me if I have any unforgiveness in my heart toward someone. I will love myself like I do my neighbor and walk the balanced life You have planned for me. Thank You for showing me one step at a time how to do it. Amen.

CHAPTER 10
Provision Through the Process

God Doesn't Call the Qualified, He Qualifies the Called

The promises of God are for you if you will receive them and take hold of them. There is a set time for your favor and a season for your breakthrough. Before the foundations of the earth were laid, God had a plan for you. His plans are without repentance and will surely come to pass in your life if you don't waiver from His path. It is out of obedience to Him that His plans are accomplished.

There is a set time and season for the blessings of God to come to you, and they fit perfectly into His plans. When God used Moses to bring the children of Israel out of Egypt, there was a set time for this to come to pass. There was a set season for Moses to walk by that burning bush and receive the instructions from God, and it was God's favor that allowed Him to come before Pharaoh and do the miracles.

TAKING YOUR TERRITORY

Are you asking the question, "Why is this happening to me?" Are you experiencing obstacles, instances where it seems like you have an "almost" breakthrough? If so, you could be walking through a wilderness experience. Promotion is easy to obtain many times, but it takes character to sustain it. There is only one way to build character, and that is through a wilderness experience.

It isn't enough to know the right thing to do or to be dedicated to what is right. Since Adam fell in the beginning of time, it caused a sin nature effect on humanity. Unfortunately, all of us have a choice to make about sin. All of us have an opportunity to do what is right, and to stop doing what is wrong.

Many times, it only takes an adjustment to our habits or way of thinking. If our thinking was developed from generation to generation, and it's just "the way it's always been done," it could possibly hinder us from moving forward into the destiny God has planned for us.

The children of Israel were indeed delivered out of Egypt from the hand of Pharaoh, but their mindset was still in slavery. They were accustomed to getting everything handed to them, being told when to work, when to eat, and what to eat. They were upset with Moses and were blaming him for bringing them into the desert because they were free. God brought freedom to them so they could believe for His hand of provision for food and water and seek His plan of destiny for them. There is a responsibility that comes with freedom.

God was training them to go into their Promised Land and receive all the blessings He was giving them. Of course, this came with giants to overcome, and relying God's provision for food, water and a place to live. They needed to trust God for everything, and this was contrary to the way they had been living for generations. Because of an entire generation refusing to change their mindset, they didn't go into the Promised Land God was leading them to. The way into the Promised Land is to seek God and be willing to change any mindset and be willing to follow His plan for everything pertaining to life.

The training for this new territory is in motion, and it's time to get ready to cross into the land of promise. What is your territory? Is it your family, your city, region, career, or business? God is preparing you take the territory He has given you for His purpose and glory. He will be with you and will never leave you nor forsake you. Facing the new challenge is the first step. This is a way you haven't been before. This is a new mindset. There are new habits to form, and old ones to stop. There are relationships you may not want to take with you into this new thing God is giving you because they aren't going the same direction as you are.

It's an exciting time where all things are becoming new. God is giving you every place where you set your foot, and no one will be able to stand against you when you put God first. The first line of action must be to establish a solid prayer life. Seeking God every day for His will and direction is first place. Our prayer life could be established with these areas of prayer:

- We enter His courts with praise each day and give thanks for all that He has given us.
- We repent for anything we are not in right-standing with Him about.
- We pray for our family, friends, and the unsaved.
- We are to pray for those in authority. This means everyone from the school principal to the president of the country.

The next thing to consider is to take responsibility for your territory. It is not by chance you are living in the neighborhood you are, working at the job you have, or going to the church you attend. Wherever you live, do business, or worship is where your territory is. It's so vital to be committed to accepting the responsibility of the territory where you are planted and be determined to accomplish the will of God for that territory.

HOW MUCH LONGER?

I am thinking of a scene in the waiting room. The doctor hasn't arrived, the nurses have other patients to attend to, and here is the mother in what seems like complete agony in childbirth. The time stands still. It feels like hours have passed, and I look at my watch, only to see twenty minutes have passed. Then, suddenly, a high-pitched cry emerges from the room as the tiny new life is welcomed.

Yes, childbirth is a process. The pregnancy of several months, waiting for the big day, the preparation of clothes, bottles, and nursery items for the new baby to be born, the watchful anticipation of the birth, then, the day finally awakens everyone to another human entering the world. The process of childbirth seems so long, and yet, the rewards are immeasurable with a new life to celebrate.

The process of birthing the dream God has put in us is much like giving birth to a child. We wait upon the Lord to give us the instructions. We begin with what we know to do and while there are growing pains, obstacles and setbacks, we continue to push through and call upon the Lord.

We stand on His Word, that He will never leave us nor forsake us. We believe in His mighty provision to bring them to pass. Yes, the process is a place of growth for us, too. We learn to trust in Him in ways we haven't before. We are taken to another level of maturity and steadiness in our walk with Him. It causes our priorities to change, and our commitment to His purposes develops deeper in obedience. We examine our motives, relationships, habits, financial spending, and how we spend our time.

There is a set time for your favor and a set season for your breakthrough. Be faithful as you journey in the process of His provision, and you will be conformed to the image of Christ.

PRAYER

Father,

Thank You for Your provisions. I know You are training me to enter the Promised Land You have for me. Help me to take responsibility for my territory and trust for You to provide everything so I can be an overcomer.

I will seek You and be willing to change my mindset to follow Your plans for my life. Help me wait on You as I grow in the process. Thank You for the favor and all the blessings You have will give me. I thank You now in advance for all You will do. Amen.

CHAPTER 11

Prayer Carves a Path to Victory

Be Joyful in Hope, Patient in Affliction, and Faithful in Prayer

Have you been on a course where you were moving along and just taking care of things, when suddenly an unexpected event came up and you didn't know what to do? It just seemed like you were minding your own business and things were moving along just fine and then something went awry that you didn't expect. I want to share a very special and interesting story of a personal unexpected experience. The outcome was amazing.

It was fall when we were moving into our new house. It was a time of joy and anticipation. Since my budget was tight at that time, I decided to rent an enclosed truck instead of hiring a moving company.

Our family had moved almost everything to the house, and I had one last load to move. Then, everyone announced that they had to go to work so now…I was solo. There were a few boxes left, some small appliances and other items that I could carry. But for a better and more efficient way of moving, I rented a dolly along with the moving truck.

I went over to get that last load of items, and when I went to pull down the large door in the back of the truck, it wouldn't lock. No matter how many times I re-opened and pulled down the door, it just wouldn't lock. I was so tired at this point that I decided to pull down the door without locking it and go ahead with finishing the move. I thought carefully about how I could just drive slowly while making the turns. After all, it was a short distance to the new house, and it would be fine with that heavy door down.

However, when I backed up into the driveway at the new house, got out of the truck and walked around to the back of the truck to open that big, heavy door, it was open, and the dolly was gone. Amazingly, all my stuff stayed in the truck.

I quickly unloaded the boxes and all the rest of the items out of the truck. I just knew that dolly was gone, since I had lost it on a busy street. I got in my car and raced back to the same streets I drove down, hoping and praying the entire time that I could find that dolly. I knew God had done miracles for me before, and I was hoping this was going to be another miracle day. The rent on the dolly was expensive, and since I was on a tight budget, it was going to be a problem if it was lost. The last thing I wanted to do was replace it.

I rehearsed in my mind what I was going to say to the rental place about how I lost that dolly, hoping they would understand. I couldn't figure out why I couldn't find it unless someone decided they needed a nice dolly. Finally, after driving around for about ten minutes, I gave up and went back home. I had resolved myself to the fact that I was going to have to explain to the rental place where that dolly went. I hoped I didn't have to buy another one for them.

I turned the corner, and there sat a red truck in front of my house with a man standing by the truck. I pulled up to the driveway and got out of my car. There stood a medium-built man with brown hair, dressed in regular, casual clothes. I looked at the kind man as he smiled back at me and asked if I could help him. He looked into my eyes, then asked me if I had lost something. His eyes were dark and had a shiny, depth to them. He reached in the back of his truck and pulled out that dolly. I was so glad to see that dolly that I was jumping up and down and thanking him. I was so happy I almost started crying.

I was thanking him and telling him I was so glad he brought that dolly back to me because it wasn't mine. He just continued to look at me and then so gently smiled as he gazed at me with his deep, piercing eyes, then asked where I wanted it. I told him to please put it in the back of the moving truck. I explained to him that the lock wasn't working, which is why the door slung open and the dolly rolled out. I asked if he could pull the heavy door down and try to get it to lock. He simply pulled down the door and locked it with ease.

He looked at me again and smiled, then asked if I needed him to do anything else. I told him thank you, but that was all, and that I appreciated him bringing it to me. I asked him how he knew to get to my house. He just smiled again while he gazed in my eyes, told me to have a good day, got back in his red truck, and drove off.

My house was in the middle of a neighborhood and was not easy to find. The only explanation I have is the kind man had to have been an angel who personally delivered that dolly to me. God was with me and in control, even when it didn't look like it with my circumstances.

While losing a dolly was a small thing in comparison to other prayer requests I have had in my life, it showed me that God cares about everything, big or small. He is interested in the details of our lives because He cares about us. He is so faithful to us.

STAY PLANTED IN HIM

God wants to share His secrets with you. He wants to share His thoughts and His heart. When a friend wants to share their secrets, the one thing they want to know is if you will keep it confidential. They want to know if they can trust you. When they call on help from you and ask for help to accomplish something, they want to know you will be there. It's all about relationship.

The people around you are watching to see how Christians live. They want to know how you are different than them, and why they need to be saved. There are so many people who leave the faith because of conflict or trials. These growing pains are just a test for your testimony.

Jesus paid a high price for you at the cross. He delivered Himself to be crucified and beaten so you may have life and healing. He suffered ridicule, being spit upon, having His beard pulled out partially and a crown of thorns placed on His head as an offering and sacrifice to bring you freedom. His love for you far out-weighs any trial you may be going through. He wants you to become all you were put on this earth to become. If He doesn't answer your prayer the way you think He should, or in your timing, will you still serve Him?

Your devotion to the Lord is the most valuable thing I can speak to you about in this book. If you don't remember anything else, just remember that your relationship with the Lord will stand against anything you face. He isn't as interested in your success as much as He is your heart.

He wants your heart.
He wants to be your first love.

PRAYING ALWAYS

One thing that is certain: when you bang on a stone hard enough and long enough, eventually it will break. The same thing is true with prayer. You are pounding the spiritual realm with Words of truth that will eventually cause a breakthrough. Every time you pray, the tide of the battle turns.

Many times, just before things turn around, the greatest battles can come up against you. This is a trick of the enemy to try and get you to quit or change your course with complaining. Instead of talking about how bad it is, start praising God and worshipping. Begin to talk about how awesome God is and how nothing is impossible with God. Get your eyes on Jesus and what He has done for you in the past.

As you mediate on His Word and think about how it declares His splendor and power, you will rise-up from the ashes of defeat in your thoughts, and those thoughts will leave. You will begin to rise-up and be strengthened as you position yourself for your victory. Battles are not won by complaining, but through praise and worship as you honor God and show forth your trust in Him.

PRAYER

Father,

Thank You for choosing me for an assignment and for the gifts You have given me to accomplish that assignment. Help me to do what is pleasing to You and not be concerned with what others think. Please give me wise mentors to be accountable to, and I will be careful to obey You. I want to follow Your instructions and not just do what everyone else is doing. Help me hear Your voice, Father.

Please help me guard my heart and to have pure motives for my service to the Kingdom of God. I want to be in right-standing with You and not do things just for eye-service. I want to stay humble, especially after my prayers are answered. Thank You for helping me. I will give You the honor and the glory for the answers to my prayers and for the victory. Amen.

CHAPTER 12
Now is the Time

Who Are You in the Kingdom of God?

I have three questions I want to ask you:

1. Who are you?
2. Where are you?
3. What time is it?

Do you know who you are in Christ? If you are born again in Christ, you are a new creature. The old has passed away, and behold, everything is new. You are born of God and carry the DNA of God. You have a unique personality, and there isn't another human being like you on this planet. You have a specific assignment that you were created to carry out. Do you realize that you are the only one with your assignment? Do you have a passion to teach? Do you desire to write or sing? What gifts do you have?

Your identity isn't wrapped up in what others say you are or who they say you are, necessarily. Take the story of Elijah being told by God to anoint Elisha to succeed him as prophet. Elijah proceeds to anoint Elisha and finds him plowing in the fields. He is working the family business. Let me first say there isn't anything wrong with carrying on a family business or helping in a family business. Elisha is fulfilling what his family wanted him to do. Think about it and pray before you overlook an opportunity that God may be presenting to you to advance His kingdom. Of course, I'm not saying to run after every opportunity that comes your way. What I am saying is not to get too comfortable in the everyday business or get so caught up in others' expectations for you that you miss your visitation from God.

Your areas of gifting and personality are wrapped in your own individual assignment in this earth. God knows you inside and out. He has placed certain gifts inside of you and knows all of your shortcomings. The very assignment you have is just as individual as your fingerprint. No one else has that job to do in this earth but you. The ministry or business is unique to you and has your fingerprint on it. The crowd of saints are peering over the balconies of heaven waiting in anticipation for you to accomplish it. Will you say, "Yes"?

When Elijah shows up to anoint Elisha, he is doing business as usual, plowing with twelve oxen. After he anoints him, Elisha wants to follow Elijah, but he tells him to go away. Imagine that!

Elisha returns, burns his plowing equipment, and has a barbecue. He feeds the people there in the village and then goes forward with his call. Before you can move forward with the call of God in your life, you need to examine some things. What is it you need to leave behind? There will be some things you need to renounce to move forward with the future God has anointed you for. There are some things or relationships you can't take with you in your future and where God is calling you.

You were meant for greatness, and nothing short of that. You were meant to be an influencer and show forth God's glory. It could be serving in ministry, owning a business, or being an accountant, plumber or public speaker. Knowing who you are in Christ keeps you from letting others define who you are.

WHERE ARE YOU?

"When they had crossed, Elijah said to Elisha, 'Tell me, what can I do for you before I am taken from you? "'Let me inherit a double portion of your spirit,' Elisha replied."[1] Can I just pause a moment and tell you, there are some things you will not get in a prayer line. You may have had a person pray over you or prophesy over you about all that God is preparing you to do, but it's not instantaneous. There is a preparation time. You may have had a prayer that you will receive a double portion, but there is a process to walk that out.

It would be like a football player getting up and going to the field to play a game and never training, working to build strength and muscle or learning the plays for the game. It takes a process to gain the spiritual strength, increase in a measure of faith, and become a vessel of honor. There are no short cuts, my friend.

God is looking for a faithful people who will serve Him in truth and honor Him with their life. It's a lifestyle of devotion to Him and not self-seeking. It's a continuous learning and training. "The student is not above their teacher, but everyone who is fully trained will be like their teacher."[2] We are to mature by constant use train ourselves to distinguish between good and evil.

Do you know where you are in the map of your life? You will know what is happening in the spirit by what you see in the natural—first the natural, then the spiritual. It is never too late to begin walking out the journey that has been predestined for you. Line upon line and precept upon precept. Here a little there a little. If you feel like you are behind schedule, just take heart. You are right on time.

WHAT TIME IS IT?

It's important to know seasons occur and to know what season you are in. Ecclesiastes says there's a time for everything. Everything has a season. Seasons of mourning. Seasons of laughter. Seasons of stretching and growing in God's plans for our lives. Seasons of abundance and blessings.

When a woman is pregnant, she goes through several months of waiting. She knows the baby is growing and is excited to think about the day when the baby will be born. She meditates on what the baby may look like and looks at other babies she sees with eager anticipation of her newborn.

As the time draws near for the birth of her child, the mother is the first to let you know. She begins to feel extremely uncomfortable as the baby gets bigger. The things she could do with ease now have become difficult. Activities must change to fit the season she is in. She needs more rest to prepare for the birth of her little blessing. She begins to nest and diligently gather the things for the baby's care needed in the first few weeks of life. She arranges the nursery and creates an environment that will be stimulating for her new bundle of joy.

She knows it is getting closer to the birth of this life inside of her. It is obvious to her that something is about to happen. She knows it. She can feel it. She has great expectation for her birthing and announces when it is time for the deliverance of this miracle of life. Even though she endures great pain to give birth, she knows that very soon she will celebrate with her blessing in her arms, as the pain melts away from the waves of joy in her heart.

This illustration is much the same with you and me. When we are believing for God to move in our life, we start out praying and believing the promises of God. We walk with God, anticipating that He will perform that which He has spoken. We meditate on His Word and sing praises to His Holy Name as we embrace Him in His presence. In the stillness and the secret of His presence, we know we are restored. We know when He calls us to come to Him, we will not refuse. For where else can we go but to the Lord?

When we don't understand this concept of seasons we can begin to lose hope and believe the season will never change. We may stop trusting or stop dreaming. As the time draws near for the Word to be manifested in our lives, we begin to experience birthing pains. We cast our cares aside. We position ourselves. We wait.

Things you once could do with ease can no longer be tolerated. The door that just closed behind you and the door that is waiting to open create an environment to prepare you for your destiny. As our eyes remain on Him, and our trust remains steady, we continue to pray, moving forward with His promises in our thoughts, words, and hearts in preparation for the answer with great expectation. Yes, the weeping and pain may endure for a night, but joy comes in the morning.

Some people who are birthing the Word of the Lord travail in prayer. Fasting and prayer right before breakthrough will usher in the Glory of God and manifest His Word. Fasting with prayer strengthens the spirit man as the focus on the spiritual becomes greater than the focus of the natural. Praying in tongues every day at least one hour a day also strengthens the spirit man.

His Word does not return unto Him void, but accomplishes that which He pleases, and it will prosper in the thing that He sent it to. Don't let the enemy move you from your peace. Keep your peace. Keep your mind stayed on Him. The distractions from the storms of life have come to lure you away from the course and cause you to grow weary. Make sure to carry this season to the fullness of time, and don't allow weariness to cause you to miscarry the promise. Stand firm—you are a child of the Most-High God. The joy of the Lord will be your strength, and He will bring you to the mountaintop victory.

"Do not fear, for I am with you; I am your God. I will strengthen you and help you. I will uphold you with my righteous right hand. For I am the Lord your God who takes hold of your right hand, and I am with you."[2]

Envision God saying, "I know the beginning from the end, and desire to fulfill all my purposes for you. Trust me and have courage. Come close to me for I will show you the path. Take my hand and do not fear."

PRAYER

Father,

Thank You for giving me a new life. I am so glad to be Your child. Father, please open my eyes and help me to see what You are doing in my life and around me. I know You are giving me direction to follow Your will, and I will hear Your voice behind me saying, "This is the way, walk in it." I ask You to give me strength to say strong and remain in You. I ask You to help me keep my mind stayed on You and thank You, Father, that I will not be moved from my peace. I sing praises to You and honor Your Name.

I will carry this season to the fullness of time and give birth to the promises You have predestined for me. I will trust You and know You are God. There is nothing impossible with You. Thank You for making all things new. Now my life song sings, "I am Yours and You are mine." I give You all honor and praise for who You are and all You have done. Amen.

ABOUT THE AUTHOR

Pamela Phillips is an author, speaker, and entrepreneur. She is dedicated to training and equipping believers to passionately pursue their purpose and destiny. Pamela's desire is to see this generation leave a legacy and fulfill their dreams to glorify God.

Pamela is committed to providing information for alternative health and wellness healing and networks with other business owners to providing their service. She has assisted several business owners with their business start-up solutions. She offers online classes for Christian spiritual growth, health, wellness, beauty, business start-up, and writing a book.

TO CONTACT THE AUTHOR:

Pamela Phillips
Mountain Top Health and Wellness
www.MTHealthandWellness.com

ENDNOTES

CHAPTER 1

1. Isaiah 51:5

CHAPTER 2

1. 3 John 1:2 (ESV)

2. 2. Mazzapica, Frankie. Used with permission. www.woodlandscelebration.com. Accessed November 2017.

3. Psalm 8:3-8 (ESV)

4. Isaiah 40:28-31 (NLT)

5. Luke 10:19

6. Jeremiah 1:5 (NLT)

CHAPTER 3

1. "Pride." *The American Heritage Dictionary of the English Language, 5th Edition*. www.thefreedictionary.com. Accessed November 2017.

CHAPTER 4

1. Numbers 14:1 (ESV)

2. 1 Samuel 30:8 (AMP)

3. Proverbs 3:34

4. John 15:5

CHAPTER 5

1. Matthew 7:24-25

CHAPTER 6

1. Hebrews 11:6

2. Proverbs 23:7 (KJV)

3. Luke 12:48

4. Philippians 3:14 (KJV)

CHAPTER 7

1. 3 John 1:2 (NLT)

2. 2 Timothy 3:2-5 (NIV)

3. Matthew 6:14-15

4. Luke 10: 2

5. Spurgeon, Charles, "100 of the Best Charles Spurgeon Quotes." *Leadership Resources,* February 11, 2018, https:// www.leadershipresources.org/blog/the-best-charles-spurgeon-quotes._Accessed November 2017.

6. Romans 12:2

7. Proverbs 4:23

8. Strong, Debbie, *7 Ways Anger Is Ruining Your Health*, November 2017, https://www.everydayhealth.com/news/ways-anger-ruining-your-health/. Accessed November 2017.

9. Leaf, Caroline PhD., "Toxic Thoughts," *Controlling Your Toxic Thoughts*, November 2017, www.drleaf.com/about/toxic-thoughts. Accessed November 2017.

10. Ecclesiastes 3:12-13 (ESV)

11. Ziglar, Zig, *Zig Ziglar Quotes*, November 2017, https://www.brainyquote.com/quotes/zig_ziglar_617780. Accessed November 2017.

CHAPTER 8

1. Kendrick, Alex, director. *Facing the Giants*. Sherwood Pictures, 2006.

2. John 16:33

CHAPTER 9

1. McKenna, Katie, "Health Benefits of Organic Foods." *Organic Foods – For Improved Human Health and Environment*, November 2017, www.1vigor.com/article/organic-foods-human-environment-health/. Accessed November 2017.

2. McKenna, Katie, "Health Benefits of Organic Foods." *Organic Foods – For Improved Human Health and Environment*, November 2017, www.1vigor.com/article/organic-foods-human-environment-health/. Accessed November 2017.

3. Dr. Axe, "Digestive Diseases." *Food Is Medicine*, February 2018, https://draxe.com/digestive-enzymes/ Accessed November 2017.

4. "Sports, Exercise and Diabetes," *Teens Health from Nemours,* November 2017, https://kidshealth.org/en/teens/sports-diabetes.html. Accessed November 2017.

5. Osmun, Rosie, "Oversleeping: the Effects and Health Risks of Sleeping Too Much." *The Huffington Post,* 6 December 2017. https://www.huffingtonpost.com/rosie-osmun/oversleeping-the-effects-and-health-risks-of-sleeping-too-much_b_9092982.html. Accessed December 2017.

6. Garner, Michael A. and Drummond, Sean P.A., "Who Are the Long Sleepers?" 28 August 2013. https://www.ncbi.nlm.nih.gov/pmc/articles/PMC3755488/. Accessed February 2018.

7. Osmun, Rosie, "Oversleeping: the Effects and Health Risks of Sleeping Too Much." *The Huffington Post,* 6 December 2017. https://www.huffingtonpost.com/rosie-osmun/oversleeping-the-effects-and-health-risks-of-sleeping-too-much_b_9092982.html. Accessed December 2017.

8. O'Conner, Anahad, "Really? Losing Sleep Reduces Your Pain Tolerance?" December 17, 2012. https://well.blogs.nytimes.com/2012/12/17/really-losing-sleep-reduces-your-pain-tolerance/. Accessed November 2017.

9. Leaf, Caroline, *Toxic Thoughts.* https://drleaf.com/blog/you-are-what-you-think-75-98-of-mental-and-physical-illnesses-come-from-our-thought-life/. Accessed April 2018.

10. Leaf, Caroline, *Toxic Thoughts.* https://drleaf.com/blog/

eliminating-toxic-thoughts-part-of-the-dirty-dozen-operating-in-perfectly-you/. May 6, 2015. Accessed November 2017.

CHAPTER 12

1. 2 Kings 2:9

2. Luke 6:40

WORKS CITED

The Bible. The Amplified Version. *BibleGateway.com,* https://
www.biblegateway.com/versions/English-Standard-Version-
ESV-Bible/. Accessed November 2017.

The Bible. English Standard Version. *BibleGateway.com,* https://
www.biblegateway.com/versions/English-Standard-Version-
ESV-Bible/. Accessed November 2017.

The Bible. King James Version. *BibleGateway.com,* https://www.
biblegateway.com/versions/King-James-Version-KJV-Bible/.
Accessed November 2017.

The Bible. New International Version. *BibleGateway.com,* www.
biblegateway.com/versions/New-International-Verison-NIV-
Bible/. Accessed November 2017.

The Bible. New Living Translation. *BibleGateway.com,* www.
biblegateway.com/versions/New-Living_Translations-NLT-
Bible/. Accessed November 2017.

Dr. Axe, "Digestive Diseases." *Food Is Medicine,* February 2018,
https://draxe.com/digestive-enzymes/. Accessed November
2017.

Garner, Michael A. and Drummond, Sean P.A., "Who Are the
Long Sleepers?" 28 August 2013. https://www.ncbi.nlm.nih.
gov/pmc/articles/PMC3755488/. Accessed February 2018.

Kendrick, Alex, director. *Facing the Giants*. Sherwood Pictures, 2006.

Leaf, Caroline, *Toxic Thoughts*. www.drleaf.com/about/toxic-thoughts. Accessed November 2017.

Leaf, Caroline, *Toxic Thoughts*. https://drleaf.com/blog/eliminating-toxic-thoughts-part-of-the-dirty-dozen-operating-in-perfectly-you/ *May 6, 2015*. Accessed November 2017.

Mazzapica, Frankie, https://woodlandscelebration.com. Used with permission. Accessed November 2017.

McKenna, Katie, "Health Benefits of Organic Foods." *Organic Foods – For Improved Human Health and Environment*, November 2017, www.1vigor.com/article/organic-foods-human-environment-health/. Accessed November 2017.

O'Conner, Anahad, "Really? Losing Sleep Reduces Your Pain Tolerance?" December 17, 2012. https://well.blogs.nytimes.com/2012/12/17/really-losing-sleep-reduces-your-pain-tolerance/. Accessed February 2018.

Osmun, Rosie, "Oversleeping: the Effects and Health Risks of Sleeping Too Much." *The Huffington Post*, 6 December 2017. https://www.huffingtonpost.com/rosie-osmun/oversleeping-the-effects-and-health-risks-of-sleeping-too-much_b_9092982.html. Accessed December 2017.

"Pride." *The American Heritage Dictionary of the English Language, 5ᵗʰ Edition*. www.thefreedictionary.com. Accessed

November 2017.

"Sports, Exercise and Diabetes," *Teens Health from Nemours,*
November 2017, https://kidshealth.org/en/teens/sports-
diabetes.html. Accessed November 2017.

Strong, Debbie, *7 Ways Anger Is Ruining Your Health,* November
2017, www.everydayhealth.com/news/ways-anger-ruining-your-
health/. Accessed November 2017.

Spurgeon, Charles, "100 of the Best Charles Spurgeon
Quotes." *Leadership Resources,* February 11, 2018, www.
leadershipresources.org/blog/the-best-charles-spurgeon-quotes.
Accessed November 2017.

Ziglar, Zig, *Zig Ziglar Quotes,* November 2017, www.
brainyquote.com/quotes/zig_ziglar_617780. Accessed
November 2017.